Journeying
Together in Christ

✠ ✠ ✠

The Report of the
Polish National Catholic-
Roman Catholic Dialogue

(1984 - 1989)

Journeying
Together in Christ

✠   ✠   ✠

The Report of the Polish National Catholic- Roman Catholic Dialogue

(1984 - 1989)

Edited by Stanislaus J. Brzana and Anthony M. Rysz

Our Sunday Visitor Publishing Division
Our Sunday Visitor, Inc.
Huntington, Indiana 46750

189

Contents

Foreword

It was in the closing months of 1981 that the first steps were taken which directly led to the ongoing dialogue between bishops of our Churches. To be sure there were earlier friendly contacts in passing between the Polish National Catholic Church and the National Conference of Catholic Bishops. The earliest date back to 1965, shortly after the Second Vatican Council. An event foreshadowing the growth of our contacts occurred at the death of His Holiness Pope Paul VI in 1978. At the invitation of Bishop Carroll McCormick, both the Prime Bishop and the Bishop of the Central Diocese of the Polish National Catholic Church participated in an ecumenical service and attended a Mass in memory of the Holy Father at the Roman Catholic Cathedral in Scranton. As Roman Catholics mourned the death of a Pope who was a courageous and humble apostle of Christian unity, the sympathetic presence of the Polish National Catholic hierarchy was felt with sincere appreciation.

In October 1980, almost two years to the date after the election of Pope John Paul II, Archbishop Ramon Torella, vice president of the Secretariat for Promoting Christian Unity, wrote to the General Secretary of the National Conference of Catholic Bishops. He wrote, as he said, "to let you know the special wish of the Holy Father regarding the relationship between the Polish National Catholic Church and the Roman Catholic Church.... The Holy Father expressed the wish that we ask your episcopal conference to make some inquiry into the relationship existing between the Polish National Catholic Church and the Roman Catholic Church in the U.S.A. and into the possibility of dialogue."

After suitable consultations on the Roman Catholic side, Bishop Ernest Unterkoefler, then chairman of the NCCB Committee for Ecumenical and Interreligious Affairs, wrote to the Prime Bishop of the PNCC, Francis Rowinski. In his letter of November 9, 1981, Bishop Unterkoefler said he was writing "in an informal way to ask whether you and your Church may be exploring ideas about ecumenical conversations with representatives of the Roman Catholic Church at the local, regional or national level." Stating that "the Polish National Catholic Church has a rich tradition and has our esteem," he added, "If you have any concrete and specific ideas about how we can journey together as Churches in the name of Christ, I shall be most grateful to hear from you."

The Prime Bishop promptly replied on November 24 saying, "I shall present your view to my brother bishops at our next conference in early December and will convey to you their overall sentiments." He related that "In principle, the Polish National Catholic Church looks favorably on ecumenical contacts with all Christian denominations insofar as these exchanges aim at a general improvement in mutual understanding."

He noted that while the PNCC had developed such exchanges with other churches, "Given the circumstances of our origin, relations with the Roman Catholic Church have not been as felicitous." Nonetheless, he expressed the thought that the PNCC bishops "probably would be happy to receive and study any specific ideas you may have" with respect to furthering relations.

This was confirmed when the Prime Bishop again wrote to Bishop Unterkoefler on December 10, 1981, two days after the meeting of the PNCC bishops, to report that "the consensus of opinion was favorable to the idea of talks between representatives of our respective Churches." Bishop Unterkoefler replied with appreciation, and thus the door was opened to the next stage: ongoing dialogue officially sponsored by the two Churches.

Further contact was maintained through correspondence as bishops were named to take part in the dialogue and other preparations necessary for its inauguration were made. During this period a lull ensued as the chairmanship of the NCCB Committee for Ecumenical and Interreligious Affairs passed from Bishop Unterkoefler to Archbishop John Whealon. By the end of 1983 and beginning of 1984, with assistance from Bishop John O'Connor, then the successor to Bishop McCormick in Scranton, preparations were underway in earnest, and the dialogue commenced on October 23, 1984, under the co-chairmanship of Bishop Anthony Rysz and Archbishop Whealon. After this first meeting Archbishop Whealon turned his chairmanship over to Bishop Stanislaus Brzana; and Bishop James Timlin, who had succeeded Bishop O'Connor in Scranton, joined the dialogue as a permanent member. Bishop Rysz was joined from the first meeting on by Bishop Joseph Nieminski. The Very Reverend Stanley Skrzypek and the Reverend John Hotchkin took part in the sessions as staff to the bishops. In addition to these original members, as the dialogue proceeded other bishops and experts joined in its work at various stages. In fact, of the six current Polish National Catholic bishops, all have taken part in at least one session, as have a similar number of Roman Catholic bishops.

While the work of dialogue progressed, other signal events were also taking place. In May 1985, at the invitation of Bishop Timlin, Prime Bishop Rowinski and Bishop Rysz along with Father Skrzypek journeyed to Rome to attend the consistory at which Archbishop John O'Connor and Archbishop Bernard Law were elevated to the Cardinalate. They were warmly greeted by Pope John Paul II, who expressed joy and gladness that they had accepted the invitation and were present. As a sign of love and symbol of unity in Christ, they presented His Holiness a chalice which had been used by Bishop Francis Hodur. At a general audience held during those days the Polish National Catholic bishops were invited to join with the Pope and other bishops in bestowing their episcopal blessing on all in attendance. There was also time for a meeting and exchange with officials of the Secretariat for Promoting Christian Unity.

Another important landmark in relations between our Churches took place in October 1986 when the General Synod of the Polish National Catholic Church met in Manchester, New Hampshire. At the invitation of the General Synod, Cardinal John Krol presented a significant address on Christian unity. This was the first time a Roman Catholic bishop spoke before the General Synod.

While these past five years have indeed been eventful ones for Polish National Catholic-Roman Catholic relations, some may ask why it has taken our Churches this long to develop this level of contact and exchange. In his 1981 letter, Bishop Rowinski alluded to an important factor when he spoke of "the circumstances of our origin." Addressing the dialogue and other members of our Churches when we met in Chicago in May 1988, Cardinal Joseph Bernardin spelled this out further when he said that we face "a division that occurred right within the American Catholic family" and that "many painful memories still remain among us."

As bishops we are keenly aware that beyond our dialogue, the arduous spiritual task of the purification of memory is one in which all the people of our Churches must share, opening our hearts and minds to one another so that they are not encrusted with bitterness despite the pain all have felt. We have, for this reason, authorized, along with our report, the publication of an account prepared by historians of our Churches of what Cardinal Bernardin termed "the sad events which brought us to go separate ways." There is pain and hurt in this record which cannot be disguised. But we believe it is important for us to develop to the extent possible a common memory of this story, one that is serene, fair, sympathetic, just to all and without imputation of motives. While these contributions by Dr. Joseph Wieczerzak and Monsignor John Gallagher are presented under their names only and do not form part of our report proper, their work has been reviewed by the bishops in dialogue and approved for publication along with our report.

Also a word must be said about the character of our report itself. As is usually the case in dialogues such as ours, commissions of the Churches holding conversations with one another do not make commitments on behalf of their Churches.

This remains for the Churches to do according to the authoritative procedures each has established. It is for this reason, as an act of accountability to our Churches, that we present our report to our authorities and our people so that further judgments may be made and guidance offered.

We do believe we could not have come this far in our dialogue had our efforts not been sustained by the prayers of our people which we have repeatedly requested from the outset. Also, from the beginning we have entrusted our work to the care and protection of the Blessed Virgin Mary, Mother of God and our Mother. Whatever healing and reconciling value others may find in our words we willingly attribute to her maternal intercession on our behalf.

Co-Chairmen:

The Right Reverend Anthony M. Rysz
Bishop of the Central Diocese
Polish National Catholic Church

The Most Reverend Stanislaus J. Brzana
Bishop of Ogdensburg
National Conference of Catholic Bishops

Feast of the Sacred Heart of Jesus
June 2, 1989

JOURNEYING TOGETHER IN CHRIST:

Summary Report Of The
Polish National Catholic-
Roman Catholic Dialogue
(1984 - 1989)

A Survey of the Findings of the Dialogue Thus Far.

When he addressed the dialogue in 1986, Prime Bishop John F. Swantek stated succinctly a conviction which we have held from the start of our sessions and one which has grown still stronger as we have worked together. He said, "The conversations between the Polish National Catholic Church and the Roman Catholic Church are a very important step in ecumenism because they bring two Churches together which have been separated by the events of history, but they have so many common characteristics in faith and liturgical expression." In our dialogue we have carefully studied these common characteristics which forge deep, underlying bonds of communion (*koinonia*) between our Churches, noting both major areas of identity or close similarity between us and, at the same time, areas of difference or distinctiveness which are also significant. We began with an extended discussion over a number of sessions focused on the sacramental life of the Church.

The Sacraments.

Both the PNCC and the RCC faithfully regard the sacraments as special gifts of Christ to His Church, outward signs instituted by Him as means of grace, wherein He acts in the power of the Spirit to nourish and strengthen the Church and be present among His faithful. Along with Orthodox Churches and all the Churches of the Union of Utrecht, the PNCC and the RCC hold seven sacraments: baptism, confirmation, penance, Eucharist, anointing of the sick, holy orders and matrimony (cf. *Nasz a Wiara — Our Faith*, by Bishop F. Hodur, Scranton, 1913, page 32).

Sacraments of Initiation: Baptism and Confirmation.

It is the common faith shared by the RCC and the PNCC that "by Baptism persons are grafted into the mystery of Christ; they die with Him, are buried with Him, and rise with Him. They receive the spirit of adoption as children 'in which we cry, Abba, Father' (Rom. 8:15) and thus become true adorers such as the Father seeks." (Vatican II *Constitution on the Divine Liturgy,* n. 6). Together we hold that through baptism, celebrated in our Churches according to the faith handed down to us from the Apostles, we are each made members of the one Mystical Body of Christ. In both our Churches not only adults but also infants are baptized. In both Churches baptism is administered by a bishop, priest or deacon.

In the PNCC, and the RCC, baptism and confirmation are counted as two closely inter-related sacraments. However, both Churches teach that confirmation completes baptism. Both Churches hold that confirmation imparts in a special way the special gift and seal of the Holy Spirit, strengthening the person confirmed to live according to the holy vocation of a Christian, and both typically confer this sacrament on young people at about the age of 12 to 15. In the PNCC as in the Latin rite of the RCC the bishops are the ordinary ministers of confirmation. However, in both Churches provision is made for priests to administer it when this is necessary or appropriate (e.g. in remote areas which the bishops cannot visit regularly, in the face of large numbers to be confirmed requiring that the bishops have further assistance, on occasion in the course of receiving an adult into membership in the Church, or in danger of death faced by one not yet confirmed).

The Eucharist.

It is evident that the Holy Eucharist holds a place of central importance in the life of both Churches and a great many parallels have been noted in both our past and present practices. The 1889 *Declaration of Utrecht*, article 6, held and taught by the bishops of the PNCC, speaks of it as "the true and central point of Catholic worship" while the Vatican II *Constitution on the Divine Liturgy*, no. 10, speaks of the liturgy culminating in the Eucharist as "the summit toward which the activity of the Church is directed (and) also the fount from which all her power flows."

To appreciate more fully how the eucharistic faith of the Union of Utrecht compares with that of the Roman Catholic Church it is helpful to see at somewhat greater length the sources just cited. This is a more complete citation from article 6 of the *Declaration of Utrecht*:

"Considering that the Holy Eucharist has always

15

been the true central point of Catholic worship, we consider it our duty to declare that we maintain with perfect fidelity the ancient Catholic doctrine concerning the Sacrament of the Altar, by believing that we receive the Body and Blood of our Saviour Jesus Christ under the species of bread and wine. The Eucharistic celebration in the Church is neither a continual repetition nor a renewal of the expiatory sacrifice which Jesus offered once for all upon the Cross; but it is a sacrifice because it is the perpetual commemoration of the sacrifice offered upon the Cross, and it is the act by which we represent upon earth and appropriate to ourselves the one offering which Jesus Christ makes in Heaven, according to the Epistle to the Hebrews, 9, 11-12, for the salvation of redeemed humanity, by appearing for us in the presence of God (Heb. 9:24). The character of the Holy Eucharist being thus understood, it is, at the same time, a sacrificial feast, by means of which the faithful in receiving the Body and Blood of our Saviour, enter into communion with one another (1 Cor. 10.17)."

And here follows the statement on the Eucharist from article 47 of the II Vatican Council *Constitution on the Divine Liturgy*:

"At the Last Supper, on the night he was betrayed, our savior instituted the eucharistic sacrifice of his Body and Blood. This he did in order to perpetuate the sacrifice of the Cross throughout the ages until he should come again, and so to entrust to his beloved Spouse, the Church, a memorial of his death and resurrection: a sacrament of love, sign of unity, a bond of charity, a paschal banquet in which Christ is consumed, the mind is filled with grace, and a pledge of future glory is given to us."

In reflecting on these texts we find in them a very close correspondence in the faith which each expresses in its own words. Though differences of linguistic usage can be found (e.g. *transsubstantiatio* — Trent, sess. XIII, cap. 4; and *przeistoczenie* — PNCC Catechism, 1944, p. 33) our experience of the lived faith and eucharistic devotion found in our Churches convinces us that ours is a shared belief that Christ in His unbounded love "did institute these holy mysteries in which spiritually and bodily, in His entire being, ... (He) abides among us" (PNCC *Canon*) under the appearances of bread and wine. Thus together we affirm that "the Holy Eucharist is the true Body and the true Blood of our Lord Jesus under the appearances of bread and wine for the nourishment of mankind for eternal life" (*Katechism*, catechism by Bishop F. Hodur, Scranton, 1920, page 32).

There is indeed a great deal of correspondence in eucharistic practice in our two Churches. Both Churches encourage the active participation of the faithful in the eucharistic liturgy and to this end celebrate the liturgy in the language of the people. In the United States today this is most commonly done in English in both Churches, though Polish is at times used in the PNCC and Latin or other languages in the RCC. Both Churches encourage the faithful to the frequent reception of Holy Communion, having prepared themselves for this with the Sacrament of Penance. In the PNCC children do not make their First Communion until the age of seven, and in the RCC not until they have reached the age of discernment, which is also generally seven. In both Churches children are encouraged to prepare themselves for this by first receiving the Sacrament of Penance. In addition to the requisite dispositions of the soul, the faithful are also enjoined to observe a fast from solid food and alcoholic beverages before receiving the Eucharist (for two hours in the case of the PNCC, for one hour in the case of the RCC). In both Churches the reception of the Eucharist is made available to the faithful not only on Sundays and Holy Days, but daily. Both Churches provide three ways for the reception of the Eucharist: 1) receiving the Sacred Host and the Most Precious Blood separately, 2) receiving by intinction, i.e. the Sacred Host dipped in the Most Precious Blood, or 3) receiving under one species, e.g. only the Sacred Host. In the PNCC the second form, reception by intinction, is the most common; whereas in the RCC reception in either the first or third form is more often the case.

Besides these commonalities, we have found the following practical differences between us. In the PNCC the minister of Holy Communion is a bishop, priest or deacon, whereas in the RCC it may be one of these or one who, though not ordained, has been commissioned by the Church to serve as a eucharistic minister. The PNCC administers the Eucharist only to members of its Church. The RCC as a general rule restricts admission to the sacraments to members of the Roman Catholic Church and to Eastern Orthodox Christians who ask to be admitted; but in certain circumstances of need will also admit individual Christians of other churches or ecclesial communities who request the sacraments with faith and are properly disposed.

Finally we have found that eucharistic devotion, i.e. the adoration of Christ in the Blessed Sacrament, continues to play an important part in the life of the PNCC, e.g. on the Feast of Corpus Christi, after the principal Mass on the first Sunday of each month, in the Procession of the Sacrament on Easter Morning, after Lenten Services such as the Stations of the Cross, after Penitential Services in Advent and Lent, after May and October devotions to Our Lady and June devotions to the Sacred Heart. Such eucharistic devotions have also been a prominent feature of the practice of the RCC in the past, but have now diminished in frequency because of the greater emphasis liturgical renewal has placed on the eucharistic celebration itself and the greater frequency with which it is celebrated. Thus, as an example, in many parishes the celebration of evening Masses on the days of Lent has taken the place of paraliturgical Lenten devotions such as the Stations of the Cross and the extra eucharistic devotions which accompanied them.

The Sacrament of Penance.

Together the RCC and the PNCC hold that Penance is the sacrament instituted by Jesus Christ in which through confession, sorrow and a strong purpose of amending our lives, sins are forgiven. It is grounded on the words of Christ: "As the Father has sent me so I also send you.... Whose sins you shall forgive, they are forgiven them" (Jn. 20:21, 23). With these words we believe Christ gave His Apostles and their lawful successors power and authority to absolve from sin those who sincerely repent of their offenses. On this there is no difference between us.

However we have found practical differences which are revealed in the forms used by our Churches for the administration of this sacrament.

The PNCC uses two forms in its penitential practice. Form I is Auricular (or private) Confession of the individual penitent to the confessor. This form, which may be used by all, is mandatory for children and youth until the age of 16. Form II is General Confession, the form more commonly used by adults. Following this form a penitential service is conducted in which all seeking the sacrament participate and all are absolved in common. This service, distinct from the penitential rite at the beginning of every Mass, consists of the following elements: invitation to repentance, a penitential hymn, prayer invoking the Holy Spirit, exhortation, examination of conscience, the confiteor, the assignment of a penance, and absolution.

The RCC, in contrast, has three forms for the administration of this sacrament. Form I is the Rite for the Reconciliation of Individual Penitents, and it corresponds to Form I of the PNCC. However, the RCC considers this to be the ordinary means of reconciliation with God and with the Church in which there takes place the healing encounter between our need and God's merciful compassion. Form II is the Rite for the Reconciliation of Several Penitents with Individual Confession and Absolution. This rite is followed at penitential services which are regularly scheduled by Roman Catholic parishes, especially during Advent and Lent, with a sufficient number of confessors present to hear the confessions and absolve each of those who come forward to receive the sacrament. Form III is the Rite for the Reconciliation of Several Penitents with General Confession and Absolution. This is similar to the PNCC Form II, but with these differences: 1) It is limited to circumstances of serious necessity. 2) It may not be received twice without an intervening individual confession of sins unless a just cause requires this. 3) It should be followed in due course by an individual confession in which each grave sin that has not previously been confessed is confessed. 4) It does not remove the obligation of each Roman Catholic to confess individually at least once a year all grave sins not previously confessed. 5) This third rite may not be publicly scheduled or announced in advance. 6) This third rite may not be used as part of any eucharistic liturgy.

The RCC admits Christians of other churches and ecclesial communities to this sacrament under the same conditions, by way of exception, whereby they are admitted to the Eucharist.

In reviewing these correspondences and practical differences, it was the conclusion of our dialogue that the difference between us is more a difference of form than of underlying intention or understanding of the sacrament itself.

The Anointing of the Sick.

Our discussion of this sacrament revealed no differences between us in matters of faith. It can be noted, however, that the administration of this sacrament by the RCC and the PNCC has undergone in recent years a notable degree of renewal in its liturgical celebration so that it can be seen more clearly by the faithful as a sacrament of the sick intended for healing and not constricted to the "last rites" for the dying. In certain RCC and PNCC parishes there are now on occasion communal services at which this sacrament is administered. The RCC admits other Christians to this sacrament upon the same conditions whereby they are, by way of exception, admitted to the Eucharist.

Holy Matrimony.

Marriage in Christ is held by both Churches to be a sacrament of the New Law given to us by the Lord. Thus the RCC holds that "The matrimonial covenant, by which a man and a woman establish between themselves a partnership of the whole of life, is by its nature ordered toward the good of spouses and the procreation and education of offspring; this covenant between baptized persons has been raised by Christ the Lord to the dignity of a sacrament" (*Code of Canon Law*, Canon 1055, 1). In the PNCC it is taught that "Matrimony is the Sacrament which makes a Christian man and woman husband and wife, gives them the grace to be faithful to each other, and to bring up their children in love and devotion to God" (Rt. Rev. Thaddeus Zielinski, *A Catechism of the Polish National Catholic Church*, p. 77).

A number of notable points of comparison emerged in the course of the dialogue. In the PNCC the priest who officiates at the wedding is regarded as the minister of the sacrament of matrimony. Marriages entered into without the presence of a priest are seen as legal unions but are not held to be sacramental marriages until the blessing of the priest has been received. In the Latin rite of the Roman Catholic Church the

22

husband and wife are regarded as the ministers of the sacrament of matrimony and the priest is the official witness of the Church. In the 1983 *Code of Canon Law*, baptized Latin rite Catholics who have not formally withdrawn from the Church (i.e. deliberately and knowingly) are obliged to marry in the presence of a priest and two other witnesses. This requirement (known as the "canonical form of marriage") must be observed for the marriage to be recognized as valid by the Roman Catholic Church. Exceptions may be granted only by a dispensation from the Roman Catholic bishop. Roman Catholic priests do confer the "nuptial blessing" at marriages, though this is seen as something distinct from the conferral of the sacrament itself. In times past the nuptial blessing was conferred only at the first marriage of a bride and was also restricted to certain times of the liturgical year, not being conferred during Advent and Lent. It is now conferred more widely.

Both Churches hold to the inviolability of marriage. In 1958 the PNCC determined that each of its dioceses would have a matrimonial court since cases of need were increasing. Before this date rare exceptions depended upon episcopal review of the case and concurrence of the Prime Bishop. Now these courts review cases and make their recommendations; then the bishops of the dioceses instruct their priests as to the direction to be taken. These rules are strictly enforced in the PNCC, and only active members of this Church may appeal to its matrimonial courts. The possible grounds for the annulment of marriage were set down in the guidelines of the 1958 Synod.

The diocesan bishop does not usually take such a direct hand in the matrimonial courts of the Roman Catholic Church.

Declarations of nullity are granted only when a case is reviewed by two successive courts and grounds have been established proving the existence of a prior block which impeded a true marriage. This must be satisfactorily proven, for marriage enjoys "the favor of the law" and thus may not be declared null without such proof. While, in the past, formal cases were quite rare in Roman Catholic matrimonial courts, there has been a marked increase in more recent times.

The increase noted by the Churches was seen by the bishops as an indication of the need to convince people of the sanctity of marriage so that they prepare themselves better for it. In the face of secularizing trends, the anonymity of urban life in which people become lost and the serious problem of teenage marriage, both the Church and families have much to do.

Attention was also given to mixed marriages between Polish National Catholics and Roman Catholics. Today both Churches provide for closer contact in preparing couples for such marriages and their celebration. Ideally the priests of both Churches should be called upon to assist in this preparation, though in practice this as yet occurs too rarely. Due to the restrictions observed with respect to sharing the Eucharist together, the celebration of these mixed marriages outside the context of the Eucharist is counseled in many instances. Special notice was made of the promise which the Roman Catholic Church asks of its members entering mixed marriage; namely, to do all that they can to see to the Catholic baptism and upbringing of future children. While it can be explained that this promise is not intended to cancel the religious duties of the PNCC partner, the PNCC bishops pointed out that it continues to constitute a real difficulty for their people. They felt it needed to be understood that a Catholic upbringing is also provided children of the Polish National Catholic Church.

Holy Orders.

It is understood that the RCC and the PNCC similarly maintain the threefold pattern of the ordained ministry, made up of bishops, presbyters and deacons; and further that both Churches regard the apostolic succession of bishops to be integral to the ordained ministry of the Church. Given this, the dialogue turned its attention to the rites which are employed by the two Churches in the ordination of bishops as well as the rites used to ordain priests and deacons. It was the conclusion of the bishops that these rites display an essential similarity. It was noted that the sacramental form used for the ordination of a bishop in the PNCC is nearly an exact Polish rendering of the Latin form used by the Roman Catholic Church prior to the reforms instituted by Pope Paul VI in 1968.

The apostolic succession of bishops as seen in light of the teachings of the II Vatican Council and those of the Polish National Catholic Church were also presented. A good deal of clarity emerged on this matter so that the bishops were able to discern that apostolic succession is not an issue in question between the Churches. It seemed clear to the Roman Catholic participants on the basis of the evidence that the bishops of the Polish National Catholic Church are validly ordained bishops in apostolic succession.

Other matters reviewed and discussed included the procedures followed by the Churches in the selection of candidates for the office and ministry of bishops. And some further questions were raised concerning the manner in which bishops exercise the authority of their office. Principal among these was the collegiality of bishops. We see the need and the desirability of discussing further the collegiality of Roman Catholic bishops with the Bishop of Rome as the head of their college as well as the fraternal links which exist between the bishops of the PNCC and other bishops of the Old Catholic Union of Utrecht.

The Word of God.

There are numerous points on which we find no disagreement between the RCC and the PNCC with respect to the Word of God. Together we hold that "Christ the Lord, in whom the entire revelation of the Most High God is summed up (cf. 2 Cor. 1:20; 3:16 4:6) commanded the apostles to preach the Gospel" (Vatican II *Constitution on Divine Revelation*, n. 7). Further we concur that "in order that the full and living Gospel might always be preserved in the church the Apostles left bishops as their successors. They gave them 'their own position of teaching authority' (St. Irenaeus, *Adv. Haer.*, III, 3, 1: *PG* 7, 848). This sacred Tradition, then, and the sacred Scripture of both Testaments are like the mirror in which the church during its pilgrim journey here on earth contemplates God, from whom she receives everything, until such time as she is brought to see Him face to face as He really is (cf. Jn 3:2)" (Vatican II, *Ibid.*). Also we agree that "the task of giving an authentic interpretation of the Word of God, whether in its written form or in the form of Tradition, has been entrusted to the living teaching office of the Church alone. Its authority in this matter is exercised in the name of Jesus Christ. Yet this Magisterium is not superior to the Word of God, but is its servant. It teaches only what has been handed on to it" (*Ibid.* n. 8).

Prizing the Word of God as one of His greatest gifts, received from Christ with the command that it be proclaimed and preached in His name throughout the world to every person, the PNCC has not hesitated in the past to speak of the Word of God heard and preached in the Church as having sacramental power (*moc sakramentalna* — Resolution of the Second Synod, 1909; in *Wiara i Wiedza*, Scranton, 1913, page 12).

For its part the RCC does not speak of the Word of God as a sacrament distinct from and along side the seven sacraments which it celebrates. It considers the proclamation of the Word of God to be an integral part of the celebration of all the seven sacraments. The Word of God permeates all the sacramental rites. To ensure that this would be realized in practice the Second Vatican Council provided for a new emphasis on preaching and a new structure for its liturgy. The Council stressed that "two parts which in a sense go to make up the Mass, viz. the liturgy of the word and the eucharistic liturgy, are so closely connected with each other that they form but one single act of worship" (*Constitution on the Sacred Liturgy*, n. 56). Because "access to Sacred Scripture ought to be open wide to the Christian faithful," (*Constitution on Divine Revelation*, n. 22) a new lectionary or book of readings has been developed for a three-year liturgical cycle providing a much wider selection of scriptural readings at Mass than the previous one-year cycle could provide. Further the Council urged that "all clerics, particularly priests of Christ and others who, as deacons or catechists, are officially engaged in the ministry of the word, should immerse themselves in the Scriptures by constant sacred reading and diligent study. For it must not happen that anyone becomes 'an empty preacher of the word to others, not being a bearer of the word in his own heart,' (St. Augustine, *Serm.* 179; *PL* 38, 966) when he ought to be sharing the boundless riches of the divine word with the faithful committed to his care, especially in the sacred liturgy" (*Constitution on Divine Revelation*, n. 24).

This having been said, while we recognize a certain difference at least in descriptive terminology used by the PNCC and the RCC, we see as well a deep point of contact beneath this formal difference. For the RCC also holds that in His Holy Word Christ makes himself present to His people with power (*Ibid*, 13, 17) and for this reason "the Church has always venerated the divine Scriptures as she venerated the Body of the Lord, in so far as she never ceases, particularly in the Sacred Liturgy, to partake of the bread of life and to offer it to the faithful from the one table of the Word of God and the Body of Christ" (*Ibid.* n. 21).

Thus while a formal difference remains, one can see in both Churches the same instinct of faith at work, cherishing and reverencing the Sacred Scriptures and acknowledging their power in our lives.

The Life to Come.

After our dialogue on the sacraments a further subject for discussion was the doctrine of the Church concerning God's universal call of all to salvation, and teachings of the Church concerning heaven, hell and purgatory. Our dialogue took into account the teachings of Sacred Scripture, the ancient creeds, the Fathers of the Church (both East and West) as well as subsequent Church tradition.

Discussion was prompted by the fact that in the past some thought there was a difference in the Churches' teachings because of differing emphasis in preaching. The Polish National Catholic Church does not wish to stress the fear of hell and damnation as a motivation for living a Christian life since in the end it could have a demoralizing effect on the people. It was made clear in this dialogue that the Polish National Catholic Church, by its positive homiletic emphasis on God's universal salvific will as well as His gracious assistance and loving mercy toward sinners, does not intend to deny any other element of Christian teaching. The Church's basic teaching may be summed up in the words of the Most Reverend Francis Hodur, the first bishop of the Polish National Catholic Church:

"I believe in final Divine justice, in future life beyond the grave which will be the further continuation of present life dependent in state and degree of perfection and happiness on our current life but before all else on the state of our soul in the last hour before death.

"I believe in immortality and happiness in eternity, in the union with God of all people of all generations and times because I believe in the Divine power of love, charity and justice, and I desire nothing other than that it should happen to me according to my faith."

In the dialogue a fundamental agreement by the Churches

in their teaching concerning heaven was ascertained. In both Churches the intercession of the saints in heaven is invoked. Further agreement exists on prayers for the deceased, including the celebration of Masses for them. Today both Churches emphasize the compassionate mercy and love of God in preaching without denying the seriousness of hell. God is just, will never punish unjustly, and wills the salvation of all. Both Churches acknowledge that fear of damnation is not the best motive for Christian living, but it is a salutary one.

Having established this much, our dialogue gave close attention to an apparent difference which surfaced in the past. Specifically this has to do with whether hell is eternal. In *A Catechism of the Polish National Catholic Church* published by the Mission Fund PNCC, one finds the question: "What of eternal punishment?" To this the answer is given: "Eternal punishment would be contrary to the wisdom, love and justice of God" (N. 169). A different teaching is found in the *Constitution on the Church* of the Second Vatican Council, where one reads: "Since we know neither the day nor the hour, we should follow the advice of the Lord and watch constantly so that when the single course of our earthly life is completed (cf. Heb. 9:27), we may merit to enter with him into the marriage feast and be numbered among the blessed (cf. Mt. 25:31-46) and not, like the wicked and slothful servants (cf. Mt. 25:36), be ordered to depart into the eternal fire (cf. Mt. 25:41), into the outer darkness where 'there will be weeping and gnashing of teeth' (Mt. 22:13 and 25:30)" (N. 48).

In considering this disparity, three factors should be taken into account. First, the catechism cited, though significant, is not a magisterial document of the PNCC. It does not carry the weight of a citation from the Second Vatican Council, for instance. Second, the dialogue is in receipt of a statement subscribed to by the six current bishops of the PNCC under date of March 1, 1988 which reads: "Maintaining the teachings of the undivided Church, we, the Bishops of the Polish National Catholic Church, in conformity with the *Declaration of Utrecht* (September 24, 1889), affirm the following: 'The Polish National Catholic Church has not taught and does not teach the so-called doctrine of Universal Salvation.' " Third, assurances have been given that catechetical materials in use by the PNCC will be in conformity with this teaching of its bishops.

We recognize that Jesus, as recorded by the New Testament, made use of the language of His time. He spoke both of *Sheol*, the dark abode of all the dead; and *Gehenna*, the postexilic Jewish idea of an eschatological place of punishment for apostate Jews and Gentile sinners where they suffered the pain of everlasting fire. From this basis Christian theology has proceeded through a complex and extended development guided by faith in the resurrection of the dead. Nonetheless, whatever may be implied by the terms "unquenchable fire" and "everlasting fire," they should not be explained away as meaningless. On this we agree, whatever further questions remain before us.

While Roman Catholics do hold to the "fire" of hell, both Churches agree that hell's greatest torment is that of immeasurable loss. Neither Church teaches that individual human beings, even those who might be damned, are annihilated and cease to exist, as some have argued on the basis of Mt. 10:28, "Be afraid of the one who can destroy both the body and the soul in Gehenna." Both Churches appreciate that the so-called "last things" are described in our teaching by eschatological imagery and that much concerning the life beyond remains unavoidably mysterious to us as long as we sojourn in this life.

Our Dialogue Thus Far.

As we look back on the path our dialogue has taken since its beginning in 1984, we find that we have thus far discovered no doctrinal obstacle that would impede the further growth of our Churches toward that unity which we believe is Christ's will (Jn. 17:21). Though we still have more to discuss, we already have much for which to be grateful. We appreciate the words which Cardinal Bernardin addressed to us in 1988:

The existence and progress of the dialogue between bishops of the Polish National Catholic and Roman Catholic Churches is a real sign of hope and source of joy for all of us. What we witness in your work is a sincere and dedicated effort to heal a division that occurred right within the American Catholic family. Therefore it touches us deeply as Catholics living in America. We know how deeply any family can be hurt by separation among its members. Many painful memories still remain among us, for the sad events which brought us to go separate ways are not long buried in the past. They are within the living memory of many, and truthfully we must admit they still hurt. To this your dialogue is an important healing force. By rekindling our hopes it helps to free us from our sad memories and to be renewed in the promise of Our Lord that through the power of His Spirit He can build up anew our unity with one another. Through the dialogue we grow in the keen realization of how much we share together in faith and in sacramental life. We recognize that together we belong to the great Catholic family. I wholeheartedly agree with what Prime Bishop Swantek said in welcoming you to your session in Buffalo two years ago: ''The conversations between the Polish National Catholic Church and Roman Catholic Church are a very important step in ecumenism because they bring together two Churches which have been separated by events of history, but they have so many common characteristics and essentials in faith and liturgical expression...''

In 1986 the General Synod of the Polish National Catholic Church welcomed Cardinal John Krol as the representative of our National Conference of Catholic Bishops. On that occasion His Eminence stressed that our efforts toward unity must be undertaken in a way that is "radically new" and in keeping with the vision of Pope John XXIII which seeks "unity in essentials — not uniformity." In pursuit of "unity with diversity" His Eminence pointed out that the II Vatican Council called upon us to go beyond a mentality seeking "return" or "absorption." He rightly stressed that "The concept of the restoration of unity does not imply inertia and expectancy on the part of the Catholic Church and a denial of their past on the part of other Christians.''

"Rather," he said, "it means a dynamic movement toward unity in which each moves toward the other by living more faithfully the valid Christian elements in each's tradition measured against and constantly renewed according to the will of Christ."

It is precisely this "dynamic movement toward unity" to which we believe the people of our Churches are called by Christ.

In behalf of Pope John Paul II, Cardinal Agostino Casaroli, Secretary of State for the Holy See, wrote to Prime Bishop Swantek on January 16, 1988. Speaking for His Holiness, the Cardinal said:

"The Holy Father has deep interest in the dialogue between the Polish National Catholic Church and the Bishops' Committee for Ecumenical and Interreligious Affairs of the U.S. National Conference of Catholic Bishops and prays for its success, so that the communion between us can be deepened. He was happy therefore to hear of your positive assessment of that dialogue, and the progress toward understanding and unity that is being made.

Many steps must be taken for the goal of unity to be reached and these must be properly discerned as we move forward. But the conviction of His Holiness is that our ecumenical goal must be nothing less that the achievement of full ecclesiastical communion; it is toward this that the Spirit is leading us. For divisions among Christians are an obstacle to the mission of preaching the Gospel and bringing to others the saving mysteries of Christ.

We cannot go back to those fateful days, decades ago, and change the difficult events which led to separation between our people. But today's new ecumenical atmosphere allows us both to see those tragic events in a new perspective, and above all to be open to the promptings of the Spirit who alone can lead us into all truth (cf. Jn. 15:26).

The new millennium that is approaching is a special Christian moment, a special time of grace. With God's help we can make use of this opportunity to focus together on Christ, and the unity of his followers for which he prayed (cf. Jn 17:21).

It remains our hope that this dialogue, which from the beginning we have entrusted to the care and protection of the Holy Mother of God, may contribute to the progress of all our people toward the great goal of unity. We commend this report to their study and reflection and ask their prayers that God may open before us the path He intends us to follow.

A Brief History Of The
Polish National Catholic Church
And Its Origins

By
Joseph W. Wieczerzak, Ph.D.
Chairman, Polish National Catholic Church
Commission on History and Archives

The Roman Catholic Church in the United States has been a Church of immigrants and their children. It has felt immigrant unrest and has heard immigrants' complaints. Irish immigrants complained about what they felt was an imbalance of French bishops and pastors. Just as they were achieving a more secure status and representation, German immigrants protested. By the 1850s, the Germans had their first representative in the American hierarchy and gained the right to have their own ethnic parishes.

The gains of the Irish and German immigrants had not been achieved solely via peaceful petition. There was, in both cases, some militancy, confrontation and threats of separation.

Within a half century of the resolution of the German discontent, the Poles emerged as the largest discontented group. In several respects, the background of their unrest was similar to that of their Irish and German immigrant predecessors. There were also similarities in their methods of protest. They, too, were to go beyond peaceful means.

Father Wenceslaus (Waclaw) Kruszka, a pioneer historian of the Polish ethnic group in America, estimated the "Polish Catholic" population of the United States in the early 1900s at over two million. Monsignor John Tracy Ellis, a foremost historian of American Roman Catholicism, put the total of *all* Catholics in the country at that time at twelve million plus. Allowing for even a one-hundred percent exaggeration in Kruszka's estimate, it might be concluded that at the turn of the century one out of every ten American Roman Catholics was of Polish birth or parentage. And there was a possibility that the ratio in heavily immigrant-populated industrial cities and their environs ran as high as one out of every five. Most accurate was this statistic: Before the year 1908, the total number of bishops of Polish birth or origin in the American Roman Catholic hierarchy was zero. It was in this statistic that the strongest root of Polish American discontent, which soon developed into dissent, was to be found.

As early as the late 1880s, Father Ignatius Barszcz drafted a suggestion to the American bishops that there be a Slavic ethnic diocese within the hierarchical structure. There was no response to this suggestion. In 1901, Father Kruszka, basing his stand on citations from the Epistles of St. Paul (1 Tm. 5:8 and Rom. 10:15) wrote a letter which was printed in the New York *Freeman's Journal* of August 3rd under the title "Polyglot Bishops for the Polyglot Dioceses." Although the American hierarchy as a whole did not react to it, the challenging letter helped give the young Wisconsin priest a prominence among his compatriots. Father Kruszka was to play a leading role in the Polish Catholic Congress, which, already in the 1880s had presented a petition to Rome for hierarchical representation. The petition did not gain any result even though the Prefect of the Congregation for the Propagation of the Faith, Miecislaus Cardinal Ledochowski, the individual who oversaw the American Church as still a missionary branch of Roman Catholicism, was himself a Pole. Part of the reason for the rejection stemmed from a lack of accurate statistical information. Part seemed to involve "bad" reports about American Poles made by some of the American bishops when they visited Rome.

What was the nature of the "bad" reports? There has been the assumption that they included concern over "independent," movements which were making headway in several Polish American communities, and were, by then, causing considerable disquietude among the American prelates.

The Polish American "independent" movements had their progenitors in individual "independent" parishes dating back to the 1870s. Causes for the rise of such parishes varied. Kruszka's detailed history, the pages of Polish language newspapers, as well as those of local English language journals, told stories of many interparochial, internecine quarrels which led to parishes cutting off from diocesan authority and/or new parishes forming outside of that authority. The turmoil peaked in the mid-1890s and early 1900s.

Initially, the term "independent" did not stem from any doctrinal or theological roots. Rather, it involved human misunderstandings and jealousies: a pastor of an extremely large parish not allowing parishioners at its territorial fringes to form a new parish; the transfer of a popular (perhaps a *young*, popular) priest; the arrival of a priest with an unpopular reputation; financial problems and burdens resulting in tensions between pastors and trustees — these were some of the likely precipitants of the "independent" parishes.

Bishops also figured in the problems behind the rise of "independentism." Some would listen to only one side of an argument — usually the pastor's. Others would sustain unpopular pastors because they had appointed them. There were impatient bishops who assumed that quarrelsomeness was a Polish trait curable with strong doses of assimilationist "Americanism." In some cases, problems were aggravated by the lack of communication between bishops and their Polish-speaking, emotionally charged flocks. All of this could exacerbate tensions, even those which the bishops did not cause.

Indeed, there were American bishops who, in the interest of peace and for the prevention of "independentism," approved the establishment of new "people-created" Polish ethnic parishes very close to existing parishes. This occurred in Chicago and in Nanticoke, Pennsylvania. Of course, a usual condition for the establishment of Roman Catholic parishes in the United States was the turning over of their property to diocesan control. This made lay people who had secured church land and built on it fearful that they were surrendering something which they should have owned.

For the most part, early "independent" parishes tended to be short-lived. Episcopal, social, and, on occasion, legal pressures sufficed to return them to diocesan control. Those which managed to survive were likely to be vulnerable to internal divisions and a dwindling membership. Their members would be ostracized from the rest of the community, sometimes on cue from pulpits. They would be cut off from acceptance by fraternal societies. Burial would be denied them and their families in cemetery plots which they had purchased in previous years. With these, as well as other obstacles, and without charismatic leadership, exciting activity and/or ties to a denomination, "independent" parishes were virtually condemned to extinction.

However, other forces were also taking shape in the *Polonia* (as the entire Polish American community was called). A strong force was a Polish nationalism outside of partitioned Poland which was being stimulated mainly by exiled veterans of revolutions against their homeland's oppressors. It culminated in 1880 with the founding of the Polish National Alliance. The Alliance was a "blanket" organization committed to working tirelessly for Poland's independence. Its membership was open to all Polish immigrants irrespective of their religious beliefs. Its leadership was secular. Almost immediately after its birth, the Alliance was challenged by some of the Polish American clergy who became instrumental in reviving a "blanket" organization known as the Polish Roman Catholic Union.

The PNA-PRCU polarization led to a type of civil war which extended to priests and parishes, and involved verbal battles in the columns of rival newspapers. From their pulpits and other forums, pro-PRCU priests condemned the PNA as Masonic, Jewish and/or socialistic. Some went to the extent of depriving PNA members of sacraments and ministrations. Some convinced their bishops that the Alliance was like the revolutionary Irish nationalist Fenian movement which the

American hierarchy had condemned just after the Civil War. All of this brought on a counterreaction and a counteroffensive from PNA quarters which included allegations of treasonable behavior against PRCU clergy. There were activists and leaders in the PNA who supported "independentism" as a counter-movement to "clericalism."

With this support, and with some charismatic leadership by a few pro-PNA priests, "independent" parishes soon linked together — via meetings, which were sometimes termed Synods — forming quasi- and full "independent" movements. Before the mid-1890s, a quasi-movement under Father Anthony Francis Kolaszewski of Cleveland included several parishes in the midwest and east. It was a quasi-movement because Father Kolaszewski held no formal authority over it, but chose to remain a pastor with "Monsignor" as his highest title. The bylaws of Kolaszewski's parish served as a model for several others. They called for congregational ownership of property, congregational election of pastors, and complete supervision of parishes by elected committees. A Polish National Church Committee, organized in Cleveland, was to try to gather all "independent" parishes into a movement. It initiated a Synod, held in August 1894, to which it invited Rene Joseph Vilatte, an itinerant "independent" bishop consecrated by Jacobites of Ceylon. Vilatte's aim was to form a multiethnic American Catholic Church. The Cleveland gathering favored an exclusively Polish ethnic ecclesiastical organization.

Chicago and Buffalo were the next centers of Polish American religious "independentism." In Chicago, there was bitter dissatisfaction with the pastorate of Father Joseph

Barzynski, brother of Father Vincent Barzynski, the Resurrectionist superior whose order had a virtual contractual monopoly over the archdiocesan Polish ethnic parishes. An exception was Holy Trinity Parish, which was located very close to Vincent Barzynski's St. Stanislaus Kostka Church. It was founded by PNA members.

Father Anthony Kozlowski, Father Joseph Barzynski's assistant, around whom the seceding group rallied, was elected bishop by a Synod. In 1897, he was consecrated in Bern by Bishop Eduard Herzog of the Swiss Christ Catholic Church, a member denomination of the European Old Catholic Union of Utrecht whose prelates possess apostolic succession. The movement under Bishop Kozlowski was identified by several names including Polish Catholic Diocese of Chicago, Polish Old Catholic, and Polish Catholic. It survived until his death in 1907. At its peak, it claimed over twenty parishes throughout the United States and one in Canada. It ended with some half-dozen parishes, mainly in Chicago and vicinity.

In 1895, "independentism" resurfaced in Buffalo, where it had manifested itself earlier in a revolt against Father John Pitass. Father Pitass had been perceived in some quarters as an autocratic pastor. Unwilling at first to have any other parish form from his very large St. Stanislaus Bishop and Martyr Parish, he eventually relented but continued to exert his influence through the title of Vicar of the Buffalo Poles to which he was appointed by Bishop James P. Ryan in 1892. The Buffalo "independents," also via a Synod, elected Father Stephen Kaminski their bishop. Kaminski, who had been ordained by Vilatte in Cleveland, was also consecrated by him in 1898. An understanding between Kaminski and his followers and Vilatte that they would submit to his authority was not kept. Instead, Bishop Kaminski came to head what was called the Polish Catholic Church. This movement, too, lasted until its leader's death (in 1911). Like the Kozlowski movement, it had its own newspaper which served for mass outreach, editorializing and polemicizing.

Scranton, in the anthracite coal mining region of Pennsylvania, was the scene of religious unrest in 1896. Dissatisfied with what they viewed as the freewheeling lifestyle and the indifference of their pastor, Father Richard Aust, and frustrated by his refusal to discuss parish finances with them, several trustees and several hundred members of Sacred Hearts of Jesus and Mary Parish protested and rioted. In the wake of the troubles, Bishop William O'Hara replaced Father Aust. However, those dissidents who did not return organized a new parish, St. Stanislaus Bishop and Martyr, and proceeded to build a church slightly over a block away from Sacred Hearts. They assumed that Bishop O'Hara would approve its existence just as he had approved the split-off Holy Trinity Parish in Nanticoke a few years before. This time, the elderly and ailing prelate did not approve. The St. Stanislaus congregation continued with the church construction. It then invited Father Francis Hodur, the pastor of the new Nanticoke parish and former assistant at Sacred Hearts, to be its pastor.

Father Hodur, who was 31 years old when he received the invitation, was born to a peasant family in the Austrian-ruled part of Poland. An excellent pupil even though he began his schooling when he was eight years of age, he received a scholarship to a prestigious secondary school (*gymnasium*) in the historic city of Cracow. He felt discrimination from some of his fellow students and a few of his teachers because of his social class. However, he associated with classmates who were largely sons of middle-class families and of professionals who had come under the influence of "Young Poland," a movement which had for its goal the uplifting of the Polish masses. The teenaged Francis felt that he would best serve the people through the theater with involvement in didactic folk drama. He tried this after his graduation, but was disillusioned with Cracow's theater world. Then, following an earlier calling still within him, he undertook studies for the priesthood.

Seminarian Hodur read not only classical literature, but also sociopolitical, including socialist, writings. He studied and was able to cite from Pope Leo XIII's 1891 social encyclical *Rerum Novarum*. Hodur was impressed by Father Stanislaw Stojalowski, a charismatic priest who led a movement (which later became a party) that was committed to work for and with the peasantry of Austrian-ruled Poland. He was active in a student society of Stojalowski's followers which was disguised as a homiletics practice group. However, it was his involvement in a seminary students' strike for better food and living conditions that probably led to his resignation and his departure for the United States the last day of 1892.

Following a brief stay at an immigrant shelter in New York, Hodur was taken under the wing of Nanticoke's venerable Father Benvenuto Gramlewicz, accepted into the Scranton Diocese, and sent to St. Vincent's Archabbey in Latrobe, Pennsylvania to complete his seminary studies. He was ordained to the priesthood in Scranton on August 19, 1893.

Father Hodur's first assignment was as assistant to Father Aust. The latter allowed him considerable leeway in organizing a parish library and dramatic society, and in editing a weekly newspaper. He endeared himself to the Sacred Hearts parishioners. They looked to him as a dedicated priest interested in their welfare, in uplifting them and inspiring Polish patriotism within them. His ecclesiastical superiors trusted him enough to assign him as administrator of Holy Family (Slovak) Parish near downtown Scranton. But, within a matter of months, he was sent, partly at Father Gramlewicz's suggestion, to the new Nanticoke parish. All the while, Father Hodur maintained contacts with several of the Sacred Hearts families who were to organize the St. Stanislaus Parish.

In March 1897, Father Hodur left his Nanticoke pastorate accepting the invitation of the secessionist Scrantonians to be their pastor. He immediately assumed the role of their leader. Within a month of his arrival he began operating a weekly newspaper, *Straz* (The Guard) with the assistance of two lay editors. He used the paper's columns to expose the negative side of some of his brother clergy, to complain about the plight of the laboring classes, and, from its first issue, to present his thoughts on a "National Church" (*Kosciol Narodowy*). He envisioned the "National Church" as part of the Roman Catholic Church if its authorities would allow: 1) parochial ownership of church property, 2) parish governance by committees elected by parishioners, 3) appointments to pastorates of priests approved by their prospective parishioners and 4) appointment of "Polish" bishops by vote of priests and laity subject to papal confirmation.

Within two years, four parishes in northeastern Pennsylvania linked themselves with St. Stanislaus as "National Churches." In early 1989, Father Hodur journeyed to

Rome to present the four-point "National Church" program. He returned confident of its eventual approval. In September, however, when it was obvious that Rome would not respond, the Coadjutor to Bishop O'Hara, Bishop Michael Hoban excommunicated, with O'Hara's approval, the already suspended priest for leading and keeping his followers in schism.

In the pages of *Straz* and in his fiery sermons, the persistent cleric launched attacks against "Irish" bishops. He also laced into what he viewed as medieval practices that had infiltrated into the Roman Catholic Church, especially what he had perceived as its stress on hell and hellfire used in order to frighten the faithful into obedience. On the other hand, Father Hodur wrote optimistically about human potential and progress. At times, he associated with socialists, seeing socialism as a means to undo the inequality which hurt workers in an era when American capitalism reached an unbridled peak.

In 1900, the "National Church" had ten parishes associated with it in varying degrees. They included congregations in Massachusetts and New Jersey as well as those in Pennsylvania. On December 16th of that year, Father Hodur called a meeting of his parishioners after having contacted both Bishop Hoban — as the new Ordinary — and the Apostolic Delegate to the United States, Archbishop Sebastiano Martinelli, regarding terms for possible reconciliation. He himself found the conditions laid out by Bishop Hoban to be harsh, and stated that he would not submit to them. His parishioners voted to stand by him. Some historians would consider this decisive event as marking the real beginning of the Polish National Catholic Church.

The lack of success on the part of a Second Polish Catholic Congress to obtain a positive response from the American hierarchy to its plea for "Polish" auxiliary bishops in some of its dioceses probably helped strengthen the Polish National cause. But then, it also lacked a bishop. Would Father Hodur, who was titled its Administrator, and who had roundly criticized "independent" bishops now seek consecration?

Straz was mute on this, but documents found in European Old Catholic archives reveal that as early as 1899 he had sought consecration through parish petitions. The Old Catholic prelates seemed to have turned down his request mainly because they had taken the position that one Old Catholic bishop per country sufficed, and that their one American bishop was Anthony Kozlowski. In 1902, Father Hodur discussed consecration with Armenian Apostolic Prelate Housep Saradjian, but that discussion also proved fruitless.

As time went on, more and more elements signifying its commitment to Polish nationalism were brought into the Church by its leader. Messianic poets who had written of Poland's sufferings as the "Christ of nations" and who prophesied her resurrection were particularly honored in church programs. Events in Polish history were commemorated in religious as well as secular observances. The epitome of nationalistic patriotic commitment to Poland, which was, at the same time, a means of making religious services understandable to the people, was Father Hodur's introduction at St. Stanislaus on Christmas Day 1901 of a Polish Mass. The introduction was carried out somewhat gradually at the Scranton and neighboring parishes. It began with one Polish Mass per month. In some outlying parishes, especially those formerly affiliated with the Kozlowski or Kaminski movements, Latin was to persist even into the 1920s.

After consulting with his clergy, Father Hodur issued a call for the Church's First Synod for September 1904. Like the Synods called previously by "independents" in Cleveland, Chicago and Buffalo, the Scranton Synod was open to all "independent" parishes and patriotic societies. It was to include delegates from parishes already attached to the Polish National Church, delegates from one still unattached parish, and representatives of fourteen Polish National Alliance lodges, which, with one exception, were all located in northeastern Pennsylvania. Also present, were observers from the Kozlowski movement.

The Synod began with a unanimous vote to break with the Roman Catholic Church. Then, it accepted a constitution for the Church written by Father Hodur. At its conclusion, it elected Father Hodur bishop. The vote was by acclamation. It gave him a mandate to enter into discussions with the Kozlowski movement for a possible merger. Although there was a decision to merge at the December 1904 Synod of the Chicago group, which Hodur and several of his priests attended, that decision, for still unknown reasons, was not to be implemented. With this, there was also an end to the possibility of his consecration by Bishop Kozlowski, a possibility at which he had hinted during an interview by a Scranton reporter just after his election.

Following Bishop Kozlowski's death in January 1907, the way appeared clear for a European Old Catholic consecration of Bishop Hodur. Supported by a document in which priests of

49

the late Chicago prelate's remnant parishes endorsed such consecration, he presented himself at the September Old Catholic Bishops' Conference in Holland and was approved over a priest (Father John Tichy) who claimed that Kozlowski had designated him as his successor. He signed the 1889 *Union of Utrecht Declaration* and by the month's end he was consecrated in Utrecht.

In the three-year interim between Bishop Hodur's election and consecration, the Polish National Catholic Church experienced several survival-threatening crises. The caliber of some of its clergy was questionable. There were individuals (particularly among the laity) who felt that the movement was not sufficiently liberal and democratic. There were others (particularly clergy) who felt that it was too liberal and too democratic. The Chicago-based management of the Polish National Alliance did not give Bishop Hodur the endorsement for which he had hoped. It decided to wait for a "Polish" Roman Catholic bishop, and its expectations were to be realized when Paul Rhode was consecrated and installed as Auxiliary Bishop of the Chicago Archdiocese in 1908.

To cope with some of the problems, and to strengthen authority, in August 1906 Bishop Hodur convened a continuation of the First Synod. The Synod was limited to delegates from the seventeen parishes of the Church and had on its agenda such items as the printing of an official Church publication (*Straz* was, at best, semi-official), the removal by the bishop of troublesome clergy (until 1906, only a Synod could suspend priests), the opening of a seminary, and clerical celibacy (an issue which had been under discussion in 1904 but which had been tabled). The Feast of Brotherly Love, which was to be commemorated the second Sunday of September, and the Feast of the Humble Shepherds, which was to be commemorated the Sunday following Christmas, were instituted by the Synod for the Church.

The Second General Synod, held in Scranton in 1909, officially adopted the name Polish National Catholic Church (*Polski Narodowy Katolicki Kosciol*) and explained that name. (Ironically, by virtue of a county court decision in a suit instituted by the Scranton Roman Catholic Diocese in 1902, the legal name of St. Stanislaus Church had to be "Polish National Reformed," and it remained as such until 1968.) Celibacy was again on the agenda, and again it was tabled. The Second General Synod recognized the Word of God as having sacramental power. There was discussion on "ecclesiastical relations" with such denominations as the Protestant Episcopal Church. The Synod also mandated the issuance of a Polish National Catholic catechism.

The year 1913 saw the convocation by Bishop Hodur of three provincial Synods (in Wilkes-Barre, Pennsylvania; Passaic, New Jersey and Chicopee, Massachusetts) which approved a Confession of Faith written by Bishop Hodur, which he explained as a restatement for modern times of the essentials of belief.

The Third General Synod of the Polish National Catholic Church — the first one held outside of Scranton — took place in 1914 in Chicago. Its first action was the adoption of the Confession of Faith. It gave Bishop Hodur the constitutional right to have assistants, titled bishop-suffragans, even though they did not actually have episcopal rank. The bishop-suffragans were to be stationed at key locations among the then-forty parishes of the Church whose territorial "spread" extended from the east coast to Minnesota and northward into Canada. Celibacy was an agenda item again. A paper weighing its positive and negative aspects was read and discussed at length. Once again, a vote on celibacy was tabled.

The Third General Synod approved three more special feast days: Institution of the Polish National Catholic Church (the second Sunday of March), Remembrance of the Polish Motherland (the second Sunday in May), and the Christian Family (the second Sunday of October). The Synod gave its approval to extend the Church to the future independent Poland. This mission was to begin soon after the end of World War I.

The Fourth General Synod, held in Scranton in 1921, adopted a symbol, banner and anthem for the Polish National Catholic Church. It also passed resolutions regarding the basis of faith, baptism and confirmation, and the sacrament of penance. This Synod also adopted a resolution abolishing mandatory clerical celibacy in the Polish National Catholic Church. It decided to do away with the confusing title of suffragan-bishop and replaced that office with the office of dean (*dziekan*), which was to be eventually replaced by that of senior priest (*senior*). A considerable amount of the Fourth Synod's time was devoted to a discussion of the Church's mission to Poland and the difficulties which it was encountering, including difficulties which stood in the way of its acceptance as a Polish denomination by the Polish government.

It was the Fifth General Synod, held in Scranton in 1924, which approved the administrative division of the Polish

National Catholic Church into dioceses. At first, there were to be four: Central, with headquarters in Scranton; Eastern which covered New York and New England with its see in Chicopee, Massachusetts; and Poland, with its see in Cracow. (Later, there was to be a Western Diocese, with headquarters in Chicago at Bishop Kozlowksi's former cathedral, and a Buffalo-Pittsburgh Diocese, with its see at the former cathedral of Bishop Kaminski. A separate Canadian Diocese, with its cathedral church in Toronto, was created in recent years.) In light of the setting up of dioceses, the Fifth General Synod also elected four bishops, including one for Lithuanian parishes. Bishop Hodur consecrated them a month after their election without co-consecrators but with notification to the bishops of the Old Catholic Union of Utrecht.

There was to be a greater increase in the number of Polish National Catholic parishes in the post-World War I period than in the period preceding the war. A possible impetus for this stemmed from the efforts of some Roman Catholic bishops, including those of Chicago, Buffalo and Brooklyn, to "Americanize" their parishes by eliminating the use of foreign languages in their churches and parochial schools. Another factor was discontent on the part of some people and groups in the American *Polonia* at the negative stance taken by Roman Catholic clergy against Josef Pilsudski, the strongman with a socialist background who took over the government of Poland. Already during World War I, Bishop Hodur and his followers had given their support to Pilsudski. An additional factor for growth was the affiliation with the Polish National Catholic Church of several holdout "independent" parishes. Because of these and other factors, the 1926 membership of the Church was probably triple that of the previous decade with a claimed total of 91 parishes and 61,574 parishioners. It was the rapid growth which did most to precipitate the creation of the Western and Buffalo-Pittsburgh Dioceses.

The missionary Church in Poland also experienced growth even as it encountered obstacles. Its petitions to be recognized as a full-fledged denomination were ignored by the government. It was to be treated in the same manner as American Protestant denominations with missionary operations in Poland (e.g. the Seventh Day Adventists, Methodists, Mormons, etc.) despite its commitment to Polish nationalism and patriotism. There was local harassment with charges of unauthorized use of Catholic liturgical vestments and furnishings, non-access to burial grounds which were under the control of Roman Catholic parishes, and even non-registration of the births, marriages and deaths of some Polish National Catholics by local offices. Added to this were internecine quarrels which resulted in defections and secessions that were sometimes accompanied by calls for the removal of "American influence."

The Sixth General Synod, held in 1931 in Buffalo, marked a sad, low point in the Polish National Catholic Church's history. A physically ill and depressed Bishop Hodur turned from his report on the state of the Church to decry declining spirituality, indifference and the management of some parishes by "immoral elements." He was sorely disappointed that his ideas for a church-wide, more devout Society of Divine Love and for a preaching Order of Priests of God's Word fell on deaf ears. Bemoaning what he felt was the Church's loss of reforming zeal, the first Prime Bishop offered to "step down."

The Synod responded with a unanimous pledge of loyalty to him and a commitment to the program he set down when the Church was organized. Then, further saddening news came in a report of delegates from Poland which told of the defection of their Ordinary, Bishop Wladyslaw Faron, who had been elected by a Polish Synod and consecrated by Bishop Hodur in Scranton.

Though almost incapacitated by diabetes and cataracts, Bishop Francis Hodur remained Prime Bishop until his death in February 1953. He preached to St. Stanislaus' parishioners via a loudspeaker from his bed nearly every Sunday and made certain that he was kept abreast of events in the Church.

The Polish National Catholic Church's Ninth General Synod, held a year after Bishop Hodur's death, adhered to his position that Polish be the sole language of the liturgy except in extenuating circumstances. Subsequent Synods have allowed for more and more English (along with some liturgical changes) until today it is in more frequent use in worship than is the original vernacular.

In the post-Hodur era, the Polish National Catholic Church has continued to maintain its ties as a member body of the Old Catholic Union of Utrecht. Its former missionary diocese in Poland became, since the early 1950s, a totally separate denomination called the Polish Catholic Church.

The Polish National Catholic Church's sacramental intercommunion with the Protestant Episcopal Church, which had been cemented by a formal agreement in 1946, was terminated by the 1978 Fifteenth General Synod as the latter Church accepted women into its priesthood.

Through a variety of factors, including improved personal

ties in the wake of the Second Vatican Council, Polish National Catholic-Roman Catholic relations have improved considerably in most recent years, facilitating discussion and dialogue.

The Polish National Catholic Church: Its Roman Catholic Origins

By
Reverend Monsignor John P. Gallagher, Ph.D.
Historian, Diocese of Scranton

In its official title, the Polish National Catholic Church professes and firmly believes itself to be truly Catholic. For it was from the Roman Catholic tradition that its beliefs and practices were inherited. While its secession was from the authority of the See of Rome, its definition was and remains determined by its assertion of apostolic succession in its ordinations to the priesthood.

No less than did its antecedents, the hierarchy of the Polish National Catholic Church has always placed an emphasis upon sacraments and liturgical celebrations. For them, the Sacrifice of the Mass is the centerpiece of the Faith. And in consequence of its conformity to its model, the Church has retained the unswerving loyalty of 250,000 members from the midwest through the northeast United States and into Canada. Through its ninety-plus years of independence, it has benefited from the obvious generosity of its faithful. The Polish National Catholic Church has successfully endured.

How the Polish National Catholic Church came into being is a matter of historical fact. Disruptive events occurred.

Presumptions prevailed. Compromises were dismissed. Satisfactory resolutions were elusive. Attitudes hardened. Polarization ensued. Sheer momentum took over. An irrevocable break resulted.

While an undeniable conflict of personalities captured the spotlight, ideological differences gradually emerged throughout the entire process. When the dust finally settled, everyone was consoled in the conviction of absolute righteousness. Principle was defined by each of the protagonists. Consequently, they simply fought for what they believed was right. In a true sense, human nature prevailed.

Understanding what occurred is necessary if only to place into perspective the sequence of happenings. As for a starting point, the changing character of the Roman Catholic Church in the United States would have to intrude into the equation.

When the Peace Treaty of Paris ended the American Revolutionary War in 1783, there were only about twenty-five thousand Catholics residing in the former colonies. The majority of them lived in Baltimore and Philadelphia. New York City was next in importance. And the remainder were to be found in scattered areas of Maryland and Virginia. But it was soon to change. With independence, America offered a safe haven for European Catholics escaping from either oppression or poverty.

It took only five years for the number of Roman Catholics in the United States to increase to the point where the Vatican's attention was warranted. On November 6, 1789, Pope Pius VI named an American Jesuit, Father John Carroll as first Bishop of the newly-created Diocese of Baltimore, Maryland. The following summer saw another milestone. On

August 15, 1790, John Carroll was ordained to the Episcopate at Lulworth Castle, England. Finally, on December 12, 1790, the work of organizing the Roman Catholic Church in the United States began in earnest. On that day, Bishop Carroll took possession of his See at Saint Peter's Pro-Cathedral, Baltimore, Maryland.

Afterwards, the challenges faced by the neophyte prelate were enormous. Every day saw the arrival of a host of new immigrants. They entered the country along a seacoast that extended 1,500 miles. The principal ports through which they passed were Philadelphia, Baltimore and New York. But Boston and Charleston got their share as well.

Then, there was the matter of language and culture. Though the United States was English in its origins and officially endorsed only that language, the early immigrant tide included Germans and French in significant numbers.

Bishop John Carroll had to reach out to all of them wherever they chose to live. In a sense it was fortunate for him that laymen generally took the initiative. Typically, when Catholics ventured into a new area, they tended to seek out each other. When there were enough of them, they organized committees for purchasing land, building a church and notifying the bishop. While most of the early Irish and English congregations legally incorporated themselves, the Germans and the French almost always did. Eventually, Bishop Carroll became involved. It was up to him to extend recognition, to regulate the actions of the trustees, to bless the church, and to provide a pastor at the earliest possible opportunity.

Through the first twenty-five years of American Catholicism, its growth was nothing short of phenomenal. The country was expanding; the population, exploding. By 1808, it was no longer possible for Bishop Carroll to reach out adequately to the members of his flock. Rome had to respond. On April 8, that same year, Pope Pius VII announced the elevation of the See of Baltimore to the rank of an Archdiocese. Its territory to the north and the west was subdivided into four new dioceses. They were: Philadelphia, Pennsylvania; New York City, New York; Boston, Massachusetts; and, Bardstown, Kentucky.

Archbishop John Carroll was thrilled with the Vatican resolution of America's needs. Up to that point, he had had his undeniable successes in guiding the Church in America through its formative years. But it was equally true that he had had his share of heartbreaks as well. His authority was challenged on a number of occasions. And in singular instances, his authority was denied. What was to become known as "Trusteeism" became apparent even before John Carroll became a bishop.

Fittingly, when he was simply the Superior of the American Missions, it was the Irish who gave him the first indication of lay assertions of power. The place was New York City; the year, 1784. An Irish Capuchin by the name of Father Charles Whelan emigrated from Ireland just in time to become the first pastor of Saint Peter's Church. A year later, another Irish Capuchin arrived, Father Andrew Nugent. Almost immediately, a popularity contest resulted. The congregation was split into two warring factions. The trustees broke the impasse. After deciding that Father Nugent was the better preacher, they ordered Father Whelan to leave New York. The latter's supporters, however, appealed to Father John Carroll, the official Superior of the American Catholic Missions. On January 25, 1786, he answered their letters, deploring the decisions of the trustees. But his advice fell on deaf ears. Before peace finally returned, he had to remove both Capuchins and assign an Irish Dominican to the pastorate. Father William O'Brien was equal to the task. By October, 1787, the embarrassment was over at last.

But while the New York situation was winding down, Philadelphia's challenge was already waiting in the wings. Though the area's Catholics had been well served by Saint Mary's Church ever since its founding in 1741, ethnic rivalries became quite pronounced through the 1780s. By 1787, it was clear that the ethnic honeymoon was nearing an end. A group of German Catholics decided that they would settle for nothing less than their own church. Despite the protests of the two priests who were serving Saint Mary's, Fathers Robert Molyneux and Francis Beeston, the would-be organizers wrote to Father John Carroll requesting the requisite permissions. Finding himself faced with a possible repetition of what had just ended in New York, he reluctantly allowed them to proceed.

The worst, as it turned out, was yet to come. In their next exchange of letters, the Philadelphia Germans refused to accept the appointment of Father Laurence Graessl. They informed the Superior of the American Catholic Missions that they had engaged the services of a German Capuchin, Father John Charles Helbron, to be their pastor. Father John Carroll's disapproval of November 24, 1787, made no impression on them.

Within the following year, the trustees sought and won

61

legal incorporation. They finished building their new church. On November 22, 1789, Holy Trinity opened its doors as the first ethnic parish in the United States. It might be noted parenthetically that the date of the founding was within the inaugural year of the Presidency of George Washington. And well before the nation's Chief Executive could publish his "Farewell Address" in 1796, Holy Trinity Church ended in a formal schism. The congregation and its trustees refused to obey the directives of Bishop John Carroll. That schism lasted from September 1796 until January 1802. In the test of wills, the Baltimore Ordinary's finally prevailed.

While the incidents in New York and in Philadelphia were the first, they were not to be the last. Throughout the nineteenth century, the American Catholic Church suffered many embarrassments, weathered any number of storms, and staunchly adhered to its cherished principles. Almost every bishop and almost every diocese was subjected at one time or another to some disruptive effort initiated by disgruntled individuals. It could have been prompted by a priest; started by a layman; or, fueled by both.

In response to provocations, the Church did not hesitate to enforce its will. No less than any nation would, the Roman Catholic religion depended upon its organizational structure not merely for survival, but more importantly for success. Laws were formulated to meet situations. And procedures were designed to siphon off discontent as well as to resolve disputes. Challenged, it had its weapons. They included such penalties as: suspension of priests, excommunication of the defiant, interdict of churches, plus a variety of other censures. These were all deemed necessary in order to preserve the teaching authority of the Bishop of Rome in particular and of all other bishops generally. For that reason alone, the Roman Catholic Church had to be assertive.

Victories, however, carried in their wakes a formidable price tag. Even though most conflicts could not have been avoided, the aftertaste was always bittersweet. Remembrance of heated passions gave rise to smoldering resentments that took decades to dissipate. For the healing process to become effective, time was essential. Only in hindsight was it possible for winners to concede that losers would be compelled to fight only when they were absolutely convinced their cause was a righteous one. Thus, despite the suspicion of malice, the reality in each confrontation was nothing other than one of honest motivation. Looked at from that standpoint, every attempt to assert some type of independent action against authority in the Roman Catholic Church was akin to David's challenge of Goliath. But in the modern-day instances, David lacked his model's biblical strengths. Invariably, insurgents lost. And equally invariably, Rome won. The penalty for being human was paying for one's mistakes.

In sharp contrast to those dismal interludes, the Roman Catholic Church in America could point to the nineteenth century as a time when it emerged from the shadows. While it began the period hardly qualifying for minority status, it ended the hundred years with an earned recognition as the largest single religious group in the United States.

Fortuitously for its growth in the interim, there were two distinctive and massive waves of immigration. As already noted, among Catholics, the Irish and Germans were quite noticeable for their numbers among the early arrivals. But in

1845, a disaster occurred in Ireland which was to affect the American Catholic Church profoundly. It was the Potato Famine. Through the next five years, hundreds of thousands fled to North America from sure death, and they survived. Subsequently, continuing economic distress contributed to an emigration pattern that would not begin to diminish until after 1890. Through those same decades, the influx of German Catholics fleeing political instability in central and northern Europe enabled them to maintain a proportionate ratio to the Irish in Catholic industrialized areas.

While the aforementioned growth was still in progress, a new trend began to emerge in 1875. It started first as a trickle and then picked up momentum in the 1880s. In the 1890s it became a veritable deluge, one that would continue unabated until restrictive immigration quotas were imposed in 1924. For the United States the impact was enormous. Whereas the first immigrant wave blended Irish and German Catholics into larger numbers of European Protestants, the newer arrivals after 1875 were almost all Catholic. Furthermore, they brought with them profound cultural and linguistic differences. These were the people from Poland, Lithuania, the Balkans and Italy. As a consequence, the Roman Catholic Church in the United States entered into a new and dynamic phase as it tried to assimilate the millions it had inherited from Europe.

If past experience had not been there to provide a guide for orderly growth, those new immigrants might have been lost to the Faith. As it happened, however, the lessons learned from Irish and German co-existence were broadened and applied as situations developed. The concept of the "ethnic parish" as distinguished from a "territorial parish" started with the founding of Holy Trinity Parish in Philadelphia in 1789. That one German Church paved the way for Rome to recognize that the melting pot in the United States of America posed special problems which, in turn, created a necessity for adaptation. No other country had any such difficulty, for in other nations everyone spoke the same language and professed the same culture. Though the papacy was to balk when an American request was made in the mid-century to establish German dioceses, it had long since accepted the notion of parochial concessions.

Thus, the years after 1875 were most exciting in the urban industrialized population centers of the midwest and northeast portions of the United States. All of a sudden, a population explosion got underway. While Polish parishes proliferated, there were also Slovak, Lithuanian and Italian congregations emerging. Adding to the cultural diversity were such recognizable groups as Magyars, Maronites, Melkites, Ukrainian Byzantines and Byzantine Ruthenians. All shared one common bond, a deep-seated belief that salvation would be attained only through the practice of the Catholic Faith. Though each nationality accepted the primacy of the Pope, they had been conditioned by their Old World experience to expect that bishops would be drawn from their own numbers.

As such, in many instances the newer immigrants were ill-prepared to cope with the reality of the Roman Catholic Church in the United States. Upon their arrival, they were thrust into the framework of existent American dioceses, where an English-speaking clergy had been in place long before 1875. In turn, these priests were the ones who ultimately became bishops. It was only natural in the United

States that most were of Irish extraction; a strong minority, of German descent.

In ordinary circumstances, the mix worked out quite well. When a bishop was apprised of the fact that yet another immigrant enclave had surfaced and was in need of the ministrations of a priest, he did his best to recognize that congregation and to supply a pastor. But the search for qualified ecclesiastics was most difficult. Without a native-born supply to turn to anywhere in America, prelates invariably had to resort to the ranks of the immigrants themselves. A good number of the priests who surfaced, however, could not produce proof that they had been ordained nor present papers from their religious superiors or bishops that they had left Europe with the necessary permissions. Still, the requests for spiritual assistance were urgent. So bishops had to improvise and take reasonable risks.

Looking back, it was a minor miracle that millions of new Catholics were integrated without incident into the ranks of the faithful in the United States. But there were the exceptions. From time to time, the human element did prevail. Just as a multitude of challenges had been mounted against the authority of bishops by Irish and German Catholics from 1786 to 1875, the likelihood of divisive conflicts was even more pronounced afterwards. Further complicating the relationships between flocks and their shepherds were the aforementioned cultural, linguistic differences. And to make matters worse, antagonisms in times of crises were fueled with accusations of racial prejudice against Irish and German bishops. To say the least, it was a trying time.

Also, among the newer immigrants, there were no

exemptions from disputes at the parish level. Pastors had to deal with two different groups. First, there was the board of trustees. Second, there were the members of the flock. While problems could develop as to the level of service a priest was giving and people could become quite dissatisfied, those difficulties could not compare with the confrontations that trustees could create. The board generally held the deed to the church and the land upon which it stood. And where finances were concerned, they usually held the purse strings. For them, the combination of the deed and treasury were convenient weapons that they used against their pastors and, ultimately, against the bishops.

Experience taught members of the Roman Catholic hierarchy to be firm when dealing with disputes that could not be resolved at the parochial level. When lawsuits brought the participants to courts of civil law, bishops had the resources to win more than their share of decisions. And when they occasionally failed, bishops had the patience to wait out the attempt of the insurgents to exploit the victory won in the courts. The rebels soon learned that the enthusiasm of their followers withered on the vine when the penalties of excommunication and/or interdict were levied. As a result, most situations ended in reconciliation.

After 1875, however, the formula was to change, particularly where one group of immigrants was involved. To a degree, those of Polish descent rewrote the book. For reasons important to themselves, they were more likely than the people of any other nationality to experience the traumatic effects of conflict in their parishes. Moreover, once the process got underway, both sides in each imbroglio became tenacious to a fault. As the facts would show, they were not averse to taking on an "Irish" or "German" bishop if that were necessary. In the heat of the moment, ecclesiastical penalties were not a deterrent.

Through the fifty years that elapsed between 1880 and 1930, the midwest and northeast sectors of the country were exposed to this new phenomenon. Time after time, outbreaks of factionalism were noted in those mostly urban areas where the Polish had settled. After a period of time, the surprise element gave way to rhetorical question, "Where next?" Though congregations had been declared by their weary bishops to be schismatic, the ripple effect continued. By 1897, the movement had jelled to the point where independent churches now created their own separate affiliations. Yet, even in the midst of their revolution, legitimacy was all-important. Fortuitously for the rebellious, their leaders were able to appeal to other schismatic churches for assistance. With such resourcefulness, two new bishops claiming apostolic succession emerged. No other nationality in the United States was able to duplicate the feat that Polish Catholic dissidents managed.

Chicago, Illinois, was the site of the first successful effort. In 1894, Father Anthony Kozlowski organized The Polish Catholic Church in America. His claim, possibly exaggerated, included eighty thousand members administered to by twenty-four priests working in twenty-six parishes with a like number of schools. But impressive as those statistics were, he knew that the Polish Catholic temperament would never settle for anything less than a validly ordained clergy. Toward that goal, he turned to the Old Catholic Church of Utrecht,

Holland, and won the approval of Bishop Eduard Herzog of Berne, Switzerland. There, on November 21, 1897, Bishop Herzog together with Bishops Gerard Gul and Theodor Weber raised Anthony Kozlowski to the rank and dignity of a bishop. Consequently, members of The Polish Catholic Church in America breathed a collective sigh of relief. They were effectively emancipated from the authority of the Roman Catholic Church and they could still practice their faith.

Meanwhile, another group headquartered in Buffalo, New York, continued its search for equal legitimacy. Called The Polish Catholic Independent Church, it was founded by Father Stephen Kaminski. He claimed jurisdiction over thirteen priests functioning in fourteen parishes serving thirty-five thousand adherents. Although those numbers were also probably exaggerated, his movement was still large enough to demand attention. And no less than their counterparts in Chicago, they too required that a bishop be their leader.

By a stroke of luck, Father Kaminski was able to locate another schismatic sect. Its name was The Old Catholic Church of America. Its leader was Joseph Rene Villatte, a self-proclaimed archbishop who resided in Green Bay, Wisconsin. His elevation to the status of a bishop had come at the hands of a defrocked Roman Catholic prelate, Bishop Francis Xavier Alvarez of Ceylon. That ordination of May 19, 1892, was sufficient justification for Archbishop Villatte to confer the same dignity on Bishop Stephen Kaminski on an undisclosed date in 1898. His successful attainment of episcopal recognition brought The Polish Catholic Independent Church into parity with its rival, The Polish Catholic Church in America.

For all intents and purposes, the field was pre-empted from further competition. The laws of supply and demand were applicable. On the one hand, the market for independent nationalist religious assertion was a limited one. Then too, despite the heady feeling of success experienced by those willing to fight freedom from traditional authority, there was a cost factor as well. Accusations averring mismanagement, abuse, venality, prejudice, and personal enrichment were likely to be countered by similar charges leveled at the accusers. Because newspapers duly reported everything said or done, opposing sides were forced to wash their dirty linens in public. Further, resorting to the courts was a time-consuming, as well as an expensive, process.

Finally, there was the quality of Polish loyalty. However much one of them might be tempted to react against a real or apparent injustice, the vast majority Polish Catholics were inclined to resolve their problems in favor of their Roman Catholic priests and bishops. When all was said and done, eighty-five to ninety percent remained faithful before, during, and after the successful independence movements in Chicago and Buffalo.

On the other hand, members of the episcopate jealously guarded their prerogatives. It would be unthinkable to expect a Roman Catholic bishop in good standing to honor any request for episcopal ordination unless authorization came from the Vatican. Likewise, those bishops who left the discipline of Roman Catholicism to enter into schism also knew how important were their individual claims to apostolic succession. By way of example, that awareness was so prized by the hierarchy of The Old Catholic Church of Utrecht, it formally notified the Holy See every time it conferred the episcopate. Practically speaking, therefore, the door was closed to interlopers.

And so, after 1898, the intent of both Bishop Anthony Kozlowski and Bishop Stephen Kaminski was to consolidate their respective footholds in Chicago and Buffalo. Each independent Church had to protect its network of affiliates from designs of its rival. Proselytizing was a real threat since there was often overlapping of parochial outlets in Illinois, Michigan, Ohio, Pennsylvania, Massachusetts and New Jersey. For the future, both independent Polish bishops were eager to expand. Should other congregations emerge into separatism, then a choice for affiliation would exist.

Little did anyone realize that the equation was neither as simple nor as stable as Bishops Kozlowski and Kaminski would have preferred. Almost at the very moment the independent Polish Churches of Chicago and Buffalo were anointed with legitimacy, a new challenger entered the spotlight. A talented young Polish immigrant priest from the Roman Catholic Diocese of Scranton, Pennsylvania, decided on March 14, 1897, to adopt the cause of a protesting group by becoming its pastor. Because he had no permission to do so, Father Francis Hodur was suspended from the practice of his priestly functions by his superior, Bishop William O'Hara.

As it turned out, the die was cast when the penalty of clerical suspension was levied. Up to that point, the unfolding events in northeastern Pennsylvania were similar to the scores of happenings elsewhere that had preceded it. Sacred Hearts Church in Scranton was the mother Church for Polish Catholics residing in the city and its surrounding towns. The combination of its pastors and its members of the board of trustees was subject to the same stresses and strains that were evident in other areas. By 1896, eleven years after its founding, Sacred Hearts parish was torn apart by its feuding animosities. Violence occurred; the police were involved; and riots had to be quelled. The aged bishop tried to restore peace, but it was too late.

Again, as had happened in the past, the dissident faction broke away, formed its own new board of trustees, became legally incorporated, bought land a block away and began to build a new church. Because they had come to know, trust and love their former assistant pastor, Father Francis Hodur, they invited him to leave his flock at Holy Trinity Church in Nanticoke in neighboring Luzerne County. It was his acceptance of that invitation without permission, on March 14, 1897, that triggered his suspension by Bishop William O'Hara. Having come to Scranton to undertake the pastorate of Saint Stanislaus Bishop and Martyr Church, he embarked upon an odyssey which made him a truly unique and controversial figure. The Roman Catholic Church disavowed him with an excommunication by Coadjutor Bishop Michael J. Hoban on September 29, 1898.

While such a penalty could not be simply dismissed, Father Francis Hodur deftly turned the pressures put on him as telling evidence of persecution. His apparent martyrdom proved a rallying cry. By 1899, The Polish National Catholic Church was a reality. Five churches in northeastern Pennsylvania accepted him as their spokesman. By 1904 and his First General Synod, he counted on a total of eleven parishes, the most recent being those acquired in Massachusetts and New Jersey.

When Bishop Anthony Kozlowski of Chicago's Polish Catholic Church in America died on January 14, 1907, the avenue to episcopal ordination was opened. Asserting himself to be the logical successor, Francis Hodur prevailed upon Archbishop Gerard Gul to approve his ascendance under the aegis of The Old Catholic Church. At the Cathedral in Utrecht, Holland, on September 29, 1907, Archbishop Gul, together with Bishops Jacob Jan Van Thiel and Bartholomew Peter Spit, consecrated him Bishop for the Polish National Catholic Church. Thereafter, the struggle for recognition was over. When Bishop Stephen Kaminski of Buffalo's Polish Catholic Independent Church passed away on September 19, 1911, Bishop Francis Hodur had the entire field to himself. His leadership was eventually to be acknowledged by well over one hundred congregations. The Polish National Catholic Church was thereby well established.

Appendix I

Sessions of the Dialogue
1984 through mid-1989

I Passaic, New Jersey
   Church of Saints Peter and Paul
   October 23, 1984

II New York, New York
    U.S. Catholic Conference Dept. of Communications
    May 7, 1985

III Scranton, Pennsylvania
     Cathedral of Saint Stanislaus, Bishop and Martyr
     November 5, 1985

IV Philadelphia, Pennsylvania
    Chancery of the Archdiocese of Philadelphia
    May 6, 1986

V Buffalo, New York
   Cathedral of the Holy Mother of the Rosary
   November 6, 1986

VI   Scranton, Pennsylvania
     Chancery of the Diocese of Scranton
     May 14, 1987

VII Carnegie, Pennsylvania
     All Saints Church
     December 12, 1987

VIII Chicago, Illinois
     Chancery of the Archdiocese of Chicago
     May 26-27, 1988

IX   Chicopee, Massachusetts
     Holy Mother of thee Rosary Church
     November 29-30, 1988

X   Washington, District of Columbia
     Washington Retreat House
     June 1-2, 1989

Participants in the Dialogue
(and sessions attended)

For the Polish National Catholic Church:

The Right Reverend Anthony M. Rysz (co-chair)
Bishop of the Central Diocese
(I - X)

The Right Reverend Joseph I. Nieminski
Bishop of the Canadian Diocese
(I - IV, VI, IX - X)

The Most Reverend Francis Rowinski
Bishop of the Buffalo-Pittsburgh Diocese
(V - IX)

The Most Reverend John F. Swantek
Prime Bishop
(V)

The Right Reverend Joseph Zawistowski
Bishop of the Diocese of Chicago
(VII)

The Right Reverend Thomas Gnat
Bishop of the Eastern Diocese
(IX)

The Very Reverend Stanley Skrzypek
(I - X)

The Very Reverend Sigmund Peplowski
(IX - X)

Dr. Joseph W. Wieczerzak
Chairman, PNCC Commission on History and Archives
(IX - X)

The Reverend A. Waine Kargul
(X)

* * *

For the National Conference of Catholic Bishops:

The Most Reverend John F. Whealon (first co-chair)
Archbishop of Hartford
Chairman of the NCCB Committee for Ecumenical and
Interreligious Affairs
(I)

The Most Reverend Stanislaus J. Brzana (second co-chair)
Bishop of Ogdensburg
(I - V, VII - X)

The Most Reverend James C. Timlin
Bishop of Scranton
(II - X)

The Most Reverend Alfred L. Abramowicz
Assistant Bishop of Chicago
(VI, VIII - IX)

The Most Reverend Thaddeus J. Jakubowski
Assistant Bishop of Chicago
(VII)

The Most Reverend Joseph F. Maguire
Bishop of Springfield, Massachusetts
(IX)

The Reverend John F. Hotchkin
Director of Ecumenical and Interreligious Affairs, NCCB
(I - X)

The Reverend Charles W. Gusmer
(II)

The Reverend Joseph F. Mytych
(VI, VIII - IX)

The Reverend Monsignor John P. Gallagher
Historian of the Diocese of Scranton
(IX - X)

Appendix II
Documentation

Letter of The Most Reverend John F. Swantek, Prime Bishop of the Polish National Catholic Church to His Holiness Pope John Paul II (November 11, 1987) / page 83

* * *

Resolution of the National Clergy Conference of the Polish National Catholic Church (November 4, 1987) / page 85

* * *

Letter of His Eminence Agostino Cardinal Casaroli, Secretary of State of the Holy See, to The Most Reverend John F. Swantek, Prime Bishop (January 16, 1988) / page 87

Polish National Catholic Church

529 East Locust Street
Scranton, Pa. 18505

John Paul II
Vatican City,
Europe

Your Holiness:

I give special thanks to God for the occasion which He provided for our meeting in Columbia, South Carolina and the uniqueness of the moment to join with others in the Ecumenical Celebration, as you made your Second Pastoral Visit to our country.

Your address to the members of the Polish National Catholic Church and to all has left a spirit of closeness in which we could feel unity in Christ.

The Word of God spoken by Your Holiness has uplifted the Christian community and strengthened the conviction that God the Holy Spirit is leading us in this Ecumenical Age.

It was a distinct pleasure to meet with Your Holiness and to exchange personal greetings. Your presence in the United States has added a new dimension to the life of the Church, but especially to that portion of it which is known as American Polonia.

Polish National Catholics have followed your visit in the

United States with a keen interest knowing that you are aware of their faith, love and devotion to God, to Jesus Christ His son, to the Blessed Mother Mary as well as to their country and the country of their ancestors and its traditions, customs and culture, for these gave birth to the Polish National Catholic Church and its growth and development.

We are grateful to the Lord for directing our paths to fruitful dialogue and discussion which was enhanced by the presence of His Eminence, John Cardinal Krol and his address which was graciously received by the XVII General Synod of the Polish National Catholic Church.

Further progress on this road to mutual understanding and Christian unity was made manifest in the resolution of the National Conference of the Bishops and Priests of the Polish National Catholic Church held in All Saints Parish, Carnegie, Pa., USA on November 4 and 5, 1987 which recommended the Dialogue Commission to present the matter of intercommunion between our two churches.

As we approach the Feast of the Nativity of Jesus Christ our Lord and Savior, I convey to you, on behalf of the Bishops, the priests and the faithful of the Polish National Catholic Church sincere greeting and prayers that the Holy Child of Bethlehem bless and keep you.

Very sincerely yours in Christ,

The Most Rev. John F. Swantek
Prime Bishop
Polish National Catholic Church

November 11, 1987

 **Polish National Catholic Church**

529 East Locust Street
Scranton, Pa. 18505

NATIONAL CLERGY CONFERENCE
November 4, 1987
All Saints Parish
Carnegie, Pa.

RESOLUTION

I move that we, the National Clergy Conference of the Polish National Catholic Church, meeting under the leadership of Prime Bishop John F. Swantek in Carnegie, Pa., on November 4 & 5, 1987 upon receiving the progress report of the dialogue between the Roman Catholic and Polish National Catholic Churches, presented by the Rt. Rev. Anthony M. Rysz, recommend our commission's representatives to present at their next session the desire on our part to further improve relationships between our two churches by establishing intercommunion. We pray that the Holy Spirit continue to direct our deliberations.

The above resolution was regularly carried and passed.
Signed by the following:

Rev. John P. Kowalczyk. Jr.
Co-Secretary, National
Clergy Conference
P.N.C.C., November 4-5, 1987

Rev. Anthony Kopka
Co-Secretary, National
Clergy Conference
P.N.C.C., November 4-5,1987

Secretariat of State
  No. 209591

January 16, 1988

Dear Bishop Swantek,
    His Holiness Pope John Paul II has asked me to convey to
you his gratitude for your kind letter of November 11, 1987.
He was happy to meet you in Columbia, South Carolina, at the
ecumenical encounter during his pastoral visit last September.
    By indicating in your letter some of the important aspects
of Christian faith which your Church holds in common with
the Catholic Church, you point to the real, though imperfect
communion which already exists between us. The Holy Father
has deep interest in the dialogue between the Polish National
Catholic Church and the Bishops' Committee for Ecumenical
and Interreligious Affairs of the U.S. National Conference of
Catholic Bishops and prays for its success, so that the
communion between us can be deepened. He was happy
therefore to hear of your positive assessment of that dialogue,
and the progress toward understanding and unity that is being
made.
    Many steps must be taken for the goal of unity to be
reached and these must be properly discerned as we move
forward. But the conviction of His Holiness is that our
ecumenical goal must be nothing less than the achievement of

full ecclesiastical communion; it is toward this that the Spirit is leading us. For divisions among Christians are an obstacle to the mission of preaching the Gospel and bringing to others the saving mysteries of Christ.

We cannot go back to those fateful days, decades ago, and change the difficult events which led to separation between our people. But today's new ecumenical atmosphere allows us both to see those tragic events in a new perspective, and above all to be open to the promptings of the Spirit who alone can lead us into all truth (*cf. Jn 15:26*).

The new millennium that is approaching is a special Christian moment, a special time of grace. With God's help we can make use of this opportunity to focus together on Christ, and the unity of his followers for which he prayed (*cf. Jn 17:21*).

His Holiness willingly assures you of his prayers for yourself and the people you serve.

Sincerely yours in Christ,

Agostino Cardinal Casaroli
Secretary of State

The Most Reverend John F. Swantek
Prime Bishop
Polish National Catholic Church

Index

Hoban, Michael J. / 47, 72
Hodur, Prime Bishop Francis / 10, 29, 44-55, 71-73
Holy Orders, the Sacrament of / 25-26
Holy Trinity Church, Philadelphia / 62-65
Hotchkin, Reverend John F. / 9, 79
- I -
Independentism, the Emergence of / 39-43, 46-50, 52-53

- J -
Jakubowski, Bishop Thaddeus J. / 79
John Paul II, Pope / 7, 10, 81, 87-88
John XXIII, Pope / 33

- K -
Kaminski, Bishop Stephen / 43-44, 49, 53, 69-71, 73
Kargul, Reverend A. Wayne / 78
Kolaszewski, Father Anthony Francis / 42
Kopka, Reverend Anthony / 85
Kowalczyk, Reverend John P., Jr. / 85
Kozlowski, Bishop Anthony / 43-44, 48-49, 53, 68-71, 73
Krol, John Cardinal / 10, 33
Kruszka, Father Wenceslaus (Waclaw) / 38

- L -
Law, Bernard Cardinal / 10
Ledochowski, Miecislaus Cardinal / 39
Leo XIII, Pope / 45
Life to Come, The / 28-32

Poland:

- Z -

Zawistowski, Bishop Joseph / 77
Zielinski, Bishop Thaddeus / 22

*Index Prepared By: Monsignor John P. Gallagher, Ph.D.,
Historian, Diocese of*